This is the story of Maria Tallchief, the daughter of an Osage Indian, who danced her way into the hearts of millions to become America's own prima ballerina. The hard realities of backstage life mingle with the magic of the world behind the footlights to bring Maria's ballet career into sharp focus.

The author understandingly portrays Maria's childhood, her secret wish to be a great dancer, the endless hours of practice, and the thrill of soloing at the Hollywood Bowl when she was just fifteen.

Personalities of the ballet world emerge as we see Maria struggle to stardom. As the Firebird she achieved the pinnacle of her success. It was all hers now—the bravas, the autographs, the flowers, as she danced her way around the world.

Maria
TALLCHIEF
American Ballerina

Maria
TALLCHIEF

AMERICAN BALLERINA

by Adèle de Leeuw

illustrated by Russell Hoover

GARRARD PUBLISHING COMPANY
Champaign, Illinois

For Elise Maria Paschen

this story of her gifted mother

Picture credits:
Dance Collection, The New York Public Library at
    Lincoln Center: p. 65
Dance News: p. 1, 11, 16, 43, 74 (both), 88, 105,
    124, 137
Dance News: Radford Bascome, p. 105 ; Melton Pippin,
    p. 121 ; Martha Swope, p. 2

Contents

1. "Show Me What You Can Do"

Betty Marie Tallchief and her sister Marjorie blinked in the strong sunlight as they came out of the Tallchief Theater.

"That was a good movie. Now let's get an ice cream cone," six-year-old Marjorie suggested. They went into a shop also owned by their father. Betty Marie, who was two years older, importantly gave their order.

The little town of Fairfax, this summer day of 1933, drowsed in the warm Oklahoma sun. It was part of the Indian reservation on which the Osage Indians lived and where, some years before, oil had been discovered. Many of the Tallchiefs' friends had become rich, and their father, Alex, had invested his oil royalties in real estate.

Licking the last of their cones, the girls approached their house. It was big and comfortable, set on a slight hill at the edge of town and surrounded by a lovely garden which was their mother's pride.

Mrs. Tallchief met them at the door. "Just time to do your piano practice, Betty Marie, before supper. And after the dishes are cleared away, I want to talk to both of you."

"Oh dear," Marjorie said. "What have we done now?"

Mrs. Tallchief smiled. "Nothing that I know of. I have a plan, and your father agrees to it. So I want you to know about it, too."

At supper, Betty Marie looked with loving eyes at her family, gathered around the table. There was her grandmother, Eliza Tallchief, sitting quiet and erect and dressed in Indian clothes, as always. Her father had been an Osage chief, and she had grown up in an Indian village. Her son, Alex, was carried on her back when he was a papoose. Often she took her grandchildren to see some of the Indian tribal dances, and Betty Marie thrilled as the figures swayed in ritual movement to the sound of drums.

Her mother, Ruth Porter Tallchief, who had come west from Kansas, was proud of her Scottish-Irish-Dutch ancestry. She had fallen in love with Alex Tallchief, a full-blooded Osage, and had married him. Their oldest child was a boy, Gerald, who was fond of horses and outdoor sports.

Betty Marie's gaze fell on Marjorie, so much like herself, with a long oval face, brown eyes, and black hair. Marjorie was her constant companion.

Finally supper was over and the dishes were cleared away. Marjorie was jumping up and down in excitement.

"What are you going to tell us, Mother?"

"For some time, girls," Mrs. Tallchief said, "I have felt that Fairfax is not the place to bring you up."

"Why not?" Marjorie interrupted.

"Because I think that you need more opportunity to develop artistically. You both are advanced in dancing, and Betty Marie has a special talent for the piano. I want you to have the best teachers there are, so we are moving to Beverly Hills, California."

Betty Marie was silent, trying to take in this momentous news. Marjorie squealed, "Beverly Hills! Hollywood! Where the movie stars live! When, when?"

"As soon as we can arrange it."

"What about you, Daddy?" Betty Marie asked suddenly.

He gave an easy shrug. "It will be a good place to perfect my golf," he grinned.

The girls were full of questions. They had their doubts. But they knew that if their mother had decided on the move, that was all there was to it.

The Tallchiefs found a comfortable house on Rexford Drive in a pleasant section of Beverly Hills. In a short time it seemed as if they had always lived there. Betty Marie knew that her

Dancing was an important part of Betty Marie's life, even at this early stage.

mother missed being the social leader of Fairfax, but, true to her nature, Mrs. Tallchief said nothing. She had decided to make a new life here.

She lost no time in finding an excellent music teacher for Betty Marie at the Los Angeles Conservatory of Music. Then she entered both girls in the ballet classes of Ernest Belcher who, she had heard, was one of the best teachers in the city.

He looked from Betty Marie to Marjorie. "Two years apart," he said, raising his eyebrows. "You look almost like twins." It was what everyone said.

"Show me what you can do," Mr. Belcher said to Betty Marie.

Her small dark face glowed as she flung out her thin arms gracefully. She raised on her toes easily and did a double pirouette. She was proud of it, and her teacher in Fairfax had been proud, too.

Mr. Belcher did not smile. He looked grim. "Whoever let her do that?" he demanded gruffly.

Mrs. Tallchief said, "She had a fine teacher who came from Tulsa. The girls performed in quite a few recitals. Betty Marie did solos—she's done a Scottish reel and a Spanish bolero—"

Mr. Belcher said firmly, "She won't do them here. If I take your daughters, Mrs. Tallchief, it will be understood that they go into the beginners' class. More than that, they must promise to forget everything they have learned so far, and do only what I say they may do."

Mrs. Tallchief agreed readily. Mr. Belcher had an air of authority about him, and he must be right. She wanted the best for her daughters.

If the girls were disappointed, they tried not to show it. Just the same, it did seem strange and a little boring to practice, day after day, lesson after lesson, at the *barre*—the long rail that ran along the studio wall. They learned to place their feet in the five positions of the ballet dancer. They did exercises to make their muscles strong and supple. They practiced, practiced, practiced.

"Ballet," said Mr. Belcher sternly, "is a form of dance that has been four centuries in the making. It is stylized; it is perfection. It must be learned, step by step."

His pupils were cautioned time and again, "There are no shortcuts." Instead, there were rules to be obeyed, hours of practice to be observed. Marjorie and Betty Marie had learned obedience at home; they had learned to live by rules and the precept that a job, to be acceptable, must be well done. They knew the meaning of discipline—a loving discipline at home—and they did not rebel now.

"My own daughter, Marge, had to go through this," Mr. Belcher told the girls one day. "She will be a good dancer, perhaps a great one. I'm glad you came to me before you were ruined forever for ballet."

Years later Betty Marie remembered his prophecy. Marge did become a famous dancer, as partner to her husband, Gower Champion.

By the time Betty Marie was twelve she had had four years of instruction under Mr. Belcher. She carried a heavy schedule. Her mother was convinced that Betty Marie would be a great pianist rather than a dancer, so she had long hours of piano practice. Her teacher had said, "She has real ability, but she will have to work very hard."

Betty Marie applied herself to her music, not because her mother wanted her to, but because she loved it. Although her first love was dancing, she wanted to do well in both. She practiced the piano twice a day—both before and after school. She was always ready for her weekly lesson, and her teacher's praise was relayed home to Mrs. Tallchief.

Sometimes Mrs. Tallchief shaped her ambition and her dreams into words. "Won't it be fun," she would say, "when you are a famous pianist, Betty Marie? You'll travel all over the world and give concerts in all the big cities!"

"Oh, yes," Betty Marie would say, chiefly because her mother wished it and she could not disappoint her. "You'll go with me, won't you?"

"Of course."

"And Daddy, too?"

Her father, when he heard this, would grin. "Not me," he said. "Gerald and I will go back to Fairfax and wait for you to come home after bowing before all the crowned heads of Europe."

When Mr. Belcher felt that the Tallchief girls had a sure knowledge of elementary ballet he allowed them to take part in a performance at their school. It was an "Indian" dance number which wasn't particularly Indian in character. Betty Marie said scornfully, "We just jumped up and down."

Much more exciting was the chance to be part of the corps de ballet—the chorus line—of the Los Angeles Civic Opera Company. Mr. Belcher had allowed a few of his best pupils to take part in the

Dressed in Indian garb, Betty Marie (top) and her sister Marjorie perform a "tribal" dance.

engagement. Betty Marie would never forget the musty vastness of the theater backstage, the thrilling sound of the orchestra tuning up, or the heady feeling of fear and excitement as she waited for her cue.

Her twelfth birthday was highlighted by a combined piano and dance recital. Mrs. Tallchief had a special costume made for Betty Marie. It was a yellow net "ballerina" ball gown. A photographer took her picture sitting at the piano. She had practiced her numbers until they were as nearly perfect as she could make them. The photograph caught her sober little face, her shy smile, her childish pointed elbows, and her big, thoughtful eyes. Mrs. Tallchief felt the picture was the first glimpse of what the years ahead might hold.

For Betty Marie the climax of the evening came in the second half of the recital. She danced—on her toes and in her frothy yellow gown—and perhaps for the first time her own wishes and dreams came forward and dominated her mind. She knew that in her heart she wanted above everything else to be a dancer.

2. "One Must Rise Above It"

A freshman classmate stopped Betty Marie in a hall of the Beverly Hills High School. "Telephone your mother after class," she said hurriedly, "and ask if you can come home with me. We could have a game of tennis and then you could stay to supper."

Betty Marie said, "Oh, I would like that! But I have piano practice—"

Her friend interrupted. "Again? I thought you practiced before school."

"I do—and again after school."

"Well, when you've finished, come on over."

"I wish I could," Betty Marie said, "but I go to

ballet class at five, and it lasts for two hours." She tried to make her voice sound a little regretful, but really she was not sorry. Ballet was the highlight of her day.

"Good heavens!" the other girl cried. "What a life! You must enjoy it to work so hard."

"I love it!" Betty Marie said, and now her voice was full and excited. "The ballet class is with Madame Nijinska, you know."

"Who's she?"

"Oh–oh, you must have heard of her! She's the sister of the famous Russian dancer, Nijinsky. He's dead, but he was as famous as Anna Pavlova. Madame is a marvelous teacher and a well-known choreographer—"

"What's a choreographer?"

"Someone who designs dances. She's done that for the Ballet Russe de Monte Carlo—"

"There's the bell," her friend said quickly. "See you!"

Betty Marie walked on slowly. Her friend wasn't really interested, it was obvious. Betty Marie had already found that it was hard to explain her own enthusiasm to her classmates. They thought she was something of a grind, and she knew they considered her serious and shy. But it didn't matter. The world she lived in, which was somewhat alien to her friends, was very real and exciting to her.

When Nijinska came to Hollywood to open a studio it had been an event. "I've had your daughters for four years," Mr. Belcher said. "I feel I shouldn't keep them any longer when someone like Nijinska is available."

Nijinska had watched the two girls perform.

"Umm," she said. "I can do something for you, both of you." Her gaze focused on Betty Marie. "You especially, little one, if you are willing to work."

Betty Marie had found no words, but her eyes answered for her.

Madame Nijinska kindled a kind of awe in Betty Marie. She wanted to please Madame, to be a credit to her. When Madame praised something she had done she was in seventh heaven. If she fumbled or was awkward, and Madame frowned, a cloud covered the sky for the rest of the day.

Mrs. Tallchief was quietly proud that her daughters were doing so well in the studio, but she did not want Betty Marie to consider ballet more important than the piano. So Betty Marie—wanting to please her mother whom she loved dearly—worked twice as hard as she might ordinarily have done. Aside from practicing the piano twice a day, she got up very early every morning to do her first dance exercises.

Madame watched her pupils carefully. She said to her more advanced students, "I want you to take additional classes with David Lichine. It is a splendid opportunity. He'll be at Nico Charisse's studio." Nico Charisse taught ballet, too, and his daughter, Cyd, was one of Madame's prize pupils.

Cyd said, when Betty Marie asked about Lichine, "He danced with Pavlova. He's fabulous! And you'll love his wife, Tatiana Riabouchinska. She was a 'baby ballerina' in the Ballet Russe some years ago. David was her partner and they fell in love and were married. Wait till you see them!"

The romance appealed to Betty Marie. Of course

they had fallen in love! He was dark and handsome and lithe, and she was blonde and beautiful.

"She's not only beautiful," Betty Marie told her mother later, "but she's so kind and sweet. He's a terror," she added thoughtfully. "I tremble when he looks at me. So does everybody else, for that matter. I suppose it's because he expects so much of us, and we want to do everything right."

Whenever a touring company came to Los Angeles, Madame took her pupils to the theater. "You must know all the ballets by heart," she said intensely. "You must get to know the music, the movements, the meaning. You must feel them!" Afterward she would take her pupils backstage to meet the dancers. It seemed she knew everyone.

Betty Marie shivered pleasurably when she met some of the principals of the Ballet Russe, the company for which Madame did choreography. The prima ballerina, Danilova, was breathtaking. And Freddie Franklin, so handsome and friendly, called Betty Marie "Ducky."

When the great Youskevitch, who had partnered many of the famous ballerinas of the world, came to the studio one day, Betty Marie could hardly breathe. He stood off to one side and watched her. "A graceful, grave child," he said to Madame. She strained her ears, but she could not hear Madame's reply.

Betty Marie basked in the knowledge that she was studying under professionals like Madame and the Lichines. The beautiful Tatiana was known for her airy dancing in *Le Coq d'Or* (*The Golden Cockerel*) and *Les Sylphides* (*The Sylphs*). "Darling Tanya," the girls called her.

Betty Marie was determined to become a dancer, even though her mother still clung to the dream of her being a pianist. Somehow it would work out, she hoped, but she did not know how.

One day Betty Marie practically flew home from class. She was fifteen, a sophomore in high school. "I'm to do a solo!" she cried breathlessly. "Madame has given me a *soliste*'s part in her *Chopin Concerto*! She's done the choreography for Chopin's E Minor Piano Concerto no. 1. Oh, I forgot to tell you—Madame's been asked to put on the ballet in the Hollywood Bowl. Isn't that thrilling?"

Betty Marie practiced as she had never practiced before. Cyd Charisse was to have a leading role, too, and Marjorie was to be in the ballet as well. Betty Marie dreamed of the coming event. The music was in her heart; now she could express it in her toes.

The night of the performance was clear and cool, a beautiful starlit night. Tier upon tier of people waited. She would do Madame proud!

And then she fell onstage! It was a horrible moment, lying prone on the hard floor, with the other dancers swirling around her. She rose swiftly and resumed her place, but the awfulness of the moment stayed with her. She wanted to cry, but pride kept her dry-eyed.

When it was over she rushed into the wings, into Madame's arms. "I ruined it!" she wailed. "It was so lovely, and I ruined it!"

"You did well," Madame said calmly. "Every dancer experiences moments of that sort."

"But my first real solo! Oh, Madame—"

"Ssh," said Madame. "The world is not yet lost. Did you never hear of Irina Baronova? She was

dancing at a command performance, before royalty. She leaped—and landed on her head!"

Betty Marie smiled faintly.

"And then there was another dancer—I forget
her name for the moment. She was dancing the
bird-woman in *The Firebird*. Her shoulder straps
broke onstage and her costume began to come
off. What to do? Fortunately, her partner had
his wits about him. He snatched some feathers
from her tutu and held them over her until she
could exit."

Betty Marie's smile broke into a giggle.

"So you see, little one, it happens everywhere.
One must rise above it. You did right...and it
may never happen again for a long time. But the
risk is always there." She shrugged. "That is part
of dancing."

Next day the newspaper critics spoke of
Miss Tallchief's dancing with kind words. It
helped soothe her wounded spirits. Just the same,
it had been a bad moment, one she would never
forget. It was her first, and Madame had warned
it might not be her last.

3. "We Might Be Able to Use You"

When Betty Marie was sixteen, a new teacher came to Nijinska's school. She was Mia Slavenska, a Yugoslav dancer with bright gold hair and pale skin. She had been a member of the Ballet Russe. Betty Marie responded to her praise, and tried in every way to please her.

"George Denham is coming in today," Mia said to Betty Marie one afternoon. He was the manager of the Ballet Russe, which was playing in the city. "I've told him about you and he wants to see you dance."

What did that mean? Betty Marie wondered. Mia said no more and Betty Marie didn't dare ask.

She felt George Denham's eyes on her in class work. Afterwards, Mia took her into a small room and asked her to dance for them privately. Mr. Denham was a businesslike man with an impassive face. Betty Marie was unable to read his expression, but his words made her heart leap.

"If you work hard," he said seriously, "if you really want to make something of your dancing, we might be able to use you in Ballet Russe. It would be a way of continuing your training. Your parents would pay for your tuition, of course, and your expenses, but you could travel with the company and the *maitre* would give you lessons. You would have a chance to become a member of the corps de ballet."

"You mean—" Betty Marie breathed, her eyes glowing.

"I mean nothing beyond that," he said, still in that serious voice. He rose to go, as if he were in a hurry and ever so slightly bored. He must have seen so many young people dance for him!

He turned in the doorway. "You would gain excellent experience in ballet work and the theater. If you mean to be a dancer, that is essential."

Betty Marie's feet were winged on the way home. "Oh, Mother, I can't believe it," she began as she told her mother the good news. Mrs. Tallchief said quietly, "You must be doing very well, if they notice you this way. But first things first, my dear. What he talks about must be in the future. You still have to finish high school."

Betty Marie finished high school the following year. There were a series of parties, and she received a precious diploma. She had been a good student and had been accepted at the University of California. Recently boys had discovered the attractive, dark-eyed girl, and she had gone on a whirl of picnics and dances. There were promises of more dates and fun during the summer.

Betty Marie was still not sure that she wanted to go to college. She did know that she wanted a summer job. To her surprise she got one as an extra in the corps de ballet of the movie, *Presenting Lily Mars.*

Marjorie was envious in a nice, sisterly fashion. "Imagine! Working with Judy Garland and seeing all those movie stars! You *would* have all the fun."

Betty Marie said, laughing, "You're doing pretty well yourself. You have so many boyfriends I don't see how you keep your dates straight."

"You have a special one, though," Marjorie was quick to say. "I like Dave, and he certainly likes you!"

Every night Marjorie insisted on knowing what had taken place on the movie lot. "Judy's fun to work with," Betty Marie said, "though of course I don't really work with her. But I get to watch her. She's so full of vitality—she just gives off sparks. I think that's why the public's crazy about her. She sings as if her whole heart was in every song." She sighed. "I'm glad we can stand around and listen ... because that's all we do mostly, stand around, waiting to be called."

That summer of 1942 was a disturbing one. The country was at war, and one by one boys with whom she had gone to parties and played tennis joined the army and came in uniform to say good-bye. Their young faces were suddenly older and more serious. Some of her classmates were becoming engaged—or getting married. Other friends were starting to work in factories or in war plants to help in the war effort.

Nijinska closed her studio and left for New York. Some of her ballets were to be performed by the Ballet Russe and she wanted to be there to prepare the dances. Mr. Lichine had signed up with a rival company, Original Ballet Russe, and would be leaving, too. Everyone, it seemed, had a new job or a new interest—except herself. What should she do?

She was still undecided when her job at the studio ended. Then, that very afternoon, something happened that settled her problem. She came home and heard her mother talking to Tatiana Riabouchinska. She rushed into the living room.

"Darling Tanya! How wonderful that you're here!"

"I've come to say good-bye," Tanya said. "I'm leaving to join David." Betty Marie's face fell.

"Don't look so sad!" Tanya said merrily. "Why don't you come, too?"

"To New York? You're teasing."

"No, I'm not. Didn't George Denham say you might try for Ballet Russe?"

"Yes, but—"

"Madame Nijinska's there now, doing choreography for them, and Mia Slavenska's back with the company, too. There couldn't be a better time."

Tanya's enthusiasm was catching. She even convinced Mrs. Tallchief that this was a marvelous opportunity for her daughter. Betty Marie watched her mother eagerly.

Mrs. Tallchief did not hestitate long. "It might be a good idea. At the very least you could have a holiday in New York before going to college. You could shop for your clothes there—that would be fun. And there are so many things you could do and see—the theater, concerts, museums—"

"I've never ridden on a subway," Betty Marie said, "or even been on a plane. Think of that! But, oh, Mother, I should hate to leave you and

Marjorie and Daddy. I might be very homesick."

"Then you can always come back," Mrs. Tall-chief said firmly. "This will only be for a short while, anyway."

The next day Betty Marie was in a whirl of preparations—saying good-bye to friends, packing suitcases, making lists of things to do, listening to last-minute advice from her family.

Rushing through the living room, she stopped abruptly to look at her piano. Gently she closed the lid. A thousand thoughts raced through her head. Was this the end of a part of her life and the beginning of another? Only time would tell, but she had a strange feeling that with that simple action she was embarking on a new career.

4. "Don't Count on Anything"

When they arrived in New York and reached the hotel where Betty Marie had planned to stay, they found that there was no room for her. "You must come home with us," Tanya said. "You can sleep on our couch, and tomorrow we'll see what we can do." So Betty Marie went home with her friends.

"I'm going to see Mr. Denham today," she told Tanya the next morning. Full of excitement, she took a taxi to the Ballet Russe headquarters. Mr. Denham's secretary said he was very busy and could not see her. Betty Marie asked if she would at least send in her name. The secretary repeated coldly, "He's too busy to see you."

"Now what?" Betty Marie thought disconsolately. Just then Tanya arrived. "Never mind—come along to the studio and watch the girls practice. I want you to meet Helen Kramer who is in the corps, a delightful girl. Maybe she will be able to help you find a place to stay."

Betty Marie and Helen became friends at once. "We'll try the Park Savoy," Helen said. "I'm at the Van Dorn—so are quite a few Ballet Russe people—but I know they have no room." Fortunately, the Park Savoy *did* have a room. "Others in the cast stay here," Helen told her, "including Freddie Franklin."

Through Helen, Betty Marie met other members of the company when they returned to the hotel after rehearsals. There were gay get-togethers each afternoon at one hotel or another. It was good to see Nijinska again, and Mia Slavenska. They introduced her to Nathalie Krassovska, a glamorous and beautiful ballerina, one of the stars of Ballet Russe.

Krassovska was everything that Betty Marie believed she herself was not. If the Ballet Russe had dancers like Danilova and Krassovska, how would she ever find a place among them? All the *solistes*, too, seemed to be either Russian or French—which was only natural considering that these were the countries in which the ballet had been developed. Then, too, it was a "Russian" company. What chance would an American have in it?

"Krassovska's not entirely Russian," Mia said. "Her father was a Scot."

"But she's so beautiful—and I'm so plain, and not Russian, and I'm too fat. I feel—I feel—"

"Yes, I know," Mia said comfortingly. "You lack experience. But how does one get experience without trying? You must get to see Mr. Denham tomorrow. And if you get into the Ballet Russe corps, you will certainly get experience! They're planning a Canadian tour, you know, and everything's up in the air. Some of the French and Russian dancers can't get across the border without an American passport or a certified visa,

because of the war. So they must find others to take their places."

"Then maybe—" Betty Marie said tentatively.

"Don't count on anything," her old teacher advised her. "Still, if you don't go to Canada, you may be taken on when the company comes back. I'll remind Denham about you whenever I can."

"I couldn't wait until the ballet returns from Canada," Betty Marie said sadly. "My parents won't let me stay in New York alone if I don't have a job or some definite plans. I'll probably have to go home and go to college."

Mia patted her shoulder. "You must try to see Denham," she repeated. "Try every day if necessary."

So Betty Marie, without too much hope, kept trying. After a week, she was about to give up when Mr. Denham's secretary told her to report to a certain address. The company director was holding auditions there.

The director's name was Jean Yazvinsky, but he was called Ivanovitch. Betty Marie studied him as girl after girl pirouetted and balanced on her toes before him. His long thin face showed nothing of what he thought, and some of the girls muttered nervously among themselves.

"We're wasting our time," one of them said to Betty Marie. Her face was sullen. "What he wants are Russian or French dancers."

Another girl grinned. "Cheer up," she said. "We may have a chance. He'll have to take *some* of us, because he needs us, and when he does we'll just change our names from American to Russian! That would be one way out!"

Although she waited until the end of the session, Betty Marie was never called to audition. It was a deep disappointment to her. She said, when she got back to the Lichines, "I wonder if it was because I had on street clothes? Perhaps he thought I had just come in with someone else."

Her practice clothes and shoes had been sent on from California, but had not yet arrived. Now she wondered when she would get another chance. The only thing that cheered her was that, in watching the girls perform, she had seen that they were asked to do the things she knew how to do very well.

Tanya said, with a positive air, "You must arrange to stay on in New York for at least a few weeks. I will look after you. Why don't you study at the School of American Ballet? Corps girls can study there for a dollar a lesson. I'm sure I can arrange that for you, even if you do not belong to the corps."

And so she did. Betty Marie found the lessons at the school excellent, for even established ballerinas practiced there. She listened avidly to stories about George Balanchine, the director. Her curiosity was piqued because she had never seen him.

"He's remarkable," Tanya told her. "No matter whether people like his work or not, he's a genius in the ballet world. And what a career he's had! He had to earn his living, you know, from the time he was practically a child, and he's been everything—a bank porter, a saddler's apprentice, a pianist for the movies. He was only twenty when he started his own touring company in Russia and put on his own ballets. One of the members was Danilova and he married her, though he's been married to Vera Zorina, now, for some years."

It seemed to Betty Marie that the Lichines knew everybody worth knowing. She saw them often and frequently had dinner with them at the Russian Tea Room near Carnegie Hall.

"Carnegie Hall—that's where Mother pictured me giving a piano recital," she said to Tanya, with a rueful smile. It made her feel wistful that she would disappoint her mother so much. But she knew now without a doubt that she would never appear there or at any other recital hall—not as a pianist. Her life would be the ballet.

Many ballet people and lovers of the dance came to the Russian Tea Room. Betty Marie drank in the talk that flowed around her. She loved the feeling that she was part of the ballet world, even though she was only on the fringe of it—an insignificant, hopeful young girl who still had to make her way among these professionals.

"There's George Balanchine," Tanya said one evening, "—at the next table."

"Which one is he?"

"The one you wouldn't think was he," Tanya said laughing. "That's Irina Baronova and her

Balanchine, noted choreographer and ballet director, was an influence on the growth of American ballet.

husband with him. Irina's husband, Germain Sevastianov, is manager of Ballet Theatre."

Betty Marie said, in excitement, "Baronova! Oh, she's the one Madame told me about—the one who leaped, and fell on her head!"

Somehow it reassured her to see this beautiful woman, so pretty and blonde and self-possessed, sitting eating her dinner with her husband and Balanchine. And so that was Balanchine! She hadn't quite imagined him that way. He was a small man, the kind of person you might pass on the street without a second glance.

The Lichines asked the others to come to their table, and Betty Marie sat enthralled while the conversation swirled around her. Most of it was in rapid Russian, and she wondered what it was about. She noticed that Balanchine, his eyes slightly veiled, his whole expression saying nothing, kept studying her. Germain Sevastianov was more outgoing in his interest. He was asking the Lichines questions about her—in Russian—and darting quick, appraising glances in her direction.

When the Balanchine party rose to go, Lichine leaned over and patted Betty Marie's cheek. "Our friend Germain was really taking you in! Now if you cannot get into Ballet Russe, you might try Germain's Ballet Theatre!"

5. "A Dancer's Life Is a Rugged One"

Helen Kramer was impressed when Betty Marie told her of the meeting at the tearoom. "You couldn't do better than try for Ballet Theatre," she said. "It started only three years ago but it's making impressive progress. The Russian companies seem to be having all kinds of troubles, and that has helped the American company."

She explained to Betty Marie how the Ballet Theatre had started. "Lucia Chase, the dancer, financed the founding of the company. You need plenty of money to get a ballet company going," Helen said knowingly, "and she had it. Of course, the talent and direction has to be there, but money is essential! New Yorkers are proud that we have an American ballet company at last."

Betty Marie began to wonder if it might not be a good idea to apply. Wouldn't she have a better chance there, as they already had many American dancers? Then suddenly a summons came from Mr. Denham's office. What he told her put everything else out of her head.

"You are to join the Canadian tour," he said abruptly, leaving Betty Marie stunned and openmouthed. "If you can learn quickly and well, if you work hard—" He left the sentence unfinished, and she knew what it implied. If she worked hard and learned well, she might become a permanent member of the company.

"It will give you experience, which you need, and when the tour is over, we may pay you a little something, depending on how well you have done."

Helen was delighted when she learned the news. She and Betty Marie could room together, and talk everything over after a performance!

Betty Marie flew around in a happy daze, getting her clothes together, and writing the good news to her family. There would be quite a number of new girls—Americans—in the company when the ballet opened in Ottawa.

Before opening night there were days of grueling rehearsals. The company was reduced in size. As a result, Betty Marie found herself rehearsing several different parts in various ballets, and wondered which she would be asked to perform first. Hard as it was, she relished the work, for she had a good memory and learned quickly.

"Some of the girls are talking about taking Russian names," Helen said one evening as they sat in their hotel room darning their toe shoes. Betty Marie had a superstition—she believed that she danced best when her toe shoes had been darned by her mother. But since her mother was far away she had to do it herself. How glad she was that Mrs. Tallchief had taught her to sew! It was going to come in handy, she knew, in keeping her clothes in order on the tour.

"Why?" Betty Marie asked now. "What's the

matter with the names they have?" She remembered that some of the girls at the audition in New York had discussed this very thing.

"Well, the impresario back in New York isn't too pleased at having a Russian ballet company with a lot of American names!" Helen laughed. "I can see his point. In fact, I've thought about changing my own to something more glamorous. Plenty of others have done it. Alice Lillian Marks, for instance, changed her name to Alicia Markova! Hilda Munnings became Lydia Sokolova. And Gertrude Tyven took her teacher's name and added a feminine ending. She's Swobodina now. Who would ever suspect she came from Brooklyn?"

The days rushed by: rehearsals, quick meals, more rehearsals, and fittings by the wardrobe mistress. At the last moment on opening night Betty Marie learned that she was to take two parts. She would be a sultan's wife in *Schéhérazade*, and then dance a minor role in *Gaîté Parisienne*. The *soliste* who usually was the sultan's wife had moved on to a more important role. It was Betty Marie's chance.

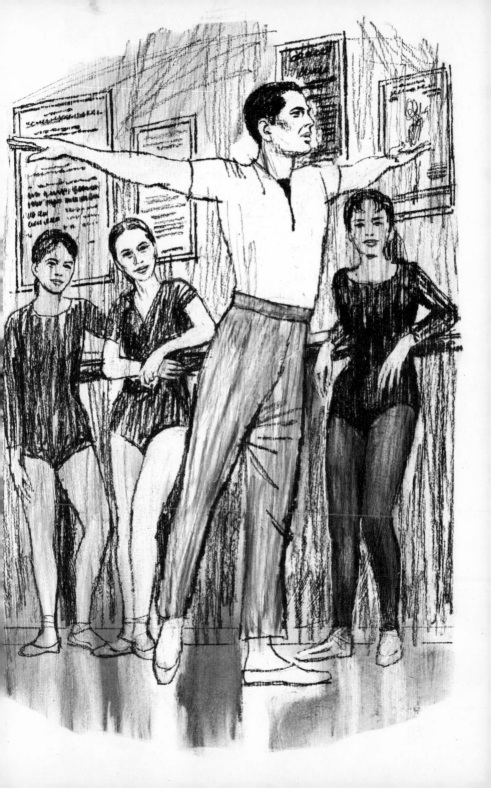

When the performance was over, and the applause had died down for the company, she sighed to herself. No one had scolded her for any mistakes, so she supposed she had done a creditable job. But she knew it was not her best. That was still to come.

The tour continued on to Montreal. The first performance there was an important one, for it was to be given for the benefit of Russian War Relief, and the governor general of Canada and his wife, Princess Alice, were to attend.

Several days before the opening, the ballet master called Betty Marie to him. "Audrey Thomas," he said, "will be taking the role of the Snow Maiden. That leaves the role of Spring free. I want you to take it."

Betty Marie was speechless. Spring was an important part—it had first been created by Alexandra Danilova, the prima ballerina of the company. This was honor indeed! She must do justice to it!

Danilova was her idol. She was everything a prima should be—lovely to look at, a superb dancer, gracious, magnetic, and a wonderful teacher. The whole company revolved around her, and she brought distinction to it. Wherever they stopped, she was greeted with flowers and luncheons. She appeared at benefits and presided over patriotic fetes. Dance lovers of each community flocked to see her. And she was as glamorous offstage as on. She glittered with beauty and energy; she was the kind of dancer Betty Marie hoped one day to be.

That first performance in Montreal went off very well. Betty Marie put her whole soul and all of her talent into being the essence of spring. When she finished she felt exhausted, yet at the same time lifted up, for she knew that she had been good.

Princess Alice came backstage. She stopped and said to Betty Marie, "I admired your dancing particularly. It was lyrical in style and spirit. You must work very hard to have learned to dance so beautifully."

Betty Marie felt the color rising in her face, making her eyes hot. She stood rooted, not quite knowing what to do or say. Should she curtsy? How did you address royalty? Should she say, "Your Highness" or "Your Grace"? She stammered something in gratitude, and the princess moved on.

Betty Marie made her way to the dressing room and sat in front of the mirror. Her face was a blur to herself, for she was looking beyond her image into the future. Was this what it might be like—this feeling of being swept up in music and movement, having your body respond to your will, reaching across the footlights to the audience and making it one with yourself? It was a heady picture, almost a frightening one.

There was a knock at the door. Startled, she said, "Come in!" and turned to see a strange man in evening dress.

He begged her pardon for intruding. "I'm manager of Canadian Concert Tours," he said, "and I just had to come back and tell you how wonderfully you danced."

"Thank you," she said gratefully.

"I hear that you're new to the company?"

"Yes, this is my first tour," Betty Marie replied.

"Then congratulations! If you go on like this, you will become one of the great ones."

"You are so kind," Betty Marie said. She felt warmed by his belief in her. She must remember his words so that she could write home about them.

Betty Marie had thought she would have opportunities to perfect her French on the tour and to go sight-seeing, but there wasn't time. They were on a tight schedule, and rehearsals came first. Some of the girls caught colds and others in the corps had to double for them. Betty Marie bent all her energies toward trying to stay well. If she became ill she knew what would happen. Her mother would tell her to come home. Her foray into the world of the ballet would be over.

It was not just the cold weather in Canada that bothered her. Little by little she became aware of a chilliness on the part of the corps girls. They didn't like her. She felt bewildered and hurt. What was it? She knew they considered her standoffish and aloof. But it was more than that.

Helen said, "They're jealous because you've been given some of the roles they would have liked. You also have more money than they do, and you spend some of it traveling Pullman when the others go by coach."

"I never thought of it," Betty Marie said in amazement. "That's the way my family always traveled. But after this, I'll go with the others."

Once or twice she overheard remarks that were made about her, and she wondered if the girls had meant her to overhear them.

"I guess it pays to have been Madame Nijinska's pupil. She's bound to get the plums."

"Oh, sure! And her father's a millionaire. He'll probably buy her her own company pretty soon."

She wouldn't answer them. She couldn't. Instead, she withdrew still further into herself. "She's just a wooden Indian," someone said.

To forget the injustice of their remarks, Betty Marie worked harder than ever. She watched avidly when the ballerinas practiced. How did they use their arms? How easy were their leaps

and pirouettes? What was the secret of their appeal? She wanted to learn everything she could, and it was a wonderful opportunity to be a part of this company and to have the chance to observe professionals at firsthand.

Traveling from place to place was hard. Her bags were heavy and she had to carry them herself. They were so heavy that they affected her arms—when she lifted them in rehearsal they were limp and painful.

"Send half your stuff home," Helen said finally. "You don't need it, and it's just a nuisance to lug around."

Betty Marie laughed. "I'm learning every day! I don't know why I didn't think of it myself. After all, most of the professionals have very little baggage, and they always look marvelous."

She packed the things she would not be wearing and shipped them home. She included the beautiful frothy robe that was too lightweight for Canada. Then she bought herself some warm underwear and a practical woolen gown. The cold was penetrating and she was not used to it.

During the rest of the short Canadian tour, when she was discouraged or tired, or when the barbs of the other girls got under her skin, she brought forth in her mind the memory of Princess Alice's words and those of the concert manager. Perhaps she would amount to something some day. But would she ever have a chance to prove herself in New York?

Several of the corps girls, annoyed that minor roles were given to Betty Marie while they still danced in the corps, went to the director and complained. In a roundabout way Betty Marie heard that the director had said, "Well, never mind. When we get back to New York, she won't have those special parts anymore. She'll be right back where the rest of you are!"

Betty Marie steeled herself against the animosity. She learned to disregard the sullen glances and the bitter words of envy.

"I'm getting toughened," she told herself in some surprise. "Perhaps this means I'm growing up!"

Betty Marie wrote her family that she was

thinking about signing up with Ballet Theatre—
if she could—when she returned to New York.
Her mother wrote back that Betty Marie would
be expected to come home to California when
Marjorie graduated. Then they could join the
same company. Perhaps Madame Nijinska or the
Lichines would form a company out there, and it
would be so pleasant to have both girls nearby.

In a few weeks the Canadian tour ended and
the tour members returned to New York. Julius
Fleischman, who was co-director of Ballet Russe
and a wealthy supporter, had been on the Canadian tour. It did not take him long to report to
Mr. Denham how well Betty Marie had performed.
He told Denham that audiences liked her and
that she had a future in ballet. Mr. Denham sent
for Betty Marie before she could see Sevastianov
at Ballet Theatre.

"We can take you into the Ballet Russe company as a regular member now," Mr. Denham
said. "You'll be on a salary, and if you work hard
and are not impatient, there will be important
roles for you. Not at first!" he warned seriously.

"Don't count on being a prima within six months!"

Betty Marie smiled faintly.

"You realize, I'm sure," he went on, "what hard work lies ahead for you." Betty Marie nodded.

"A dancer's life is a rugged one. There is constant practice and there are many disappointments," he continued. "You may have to wait a long time for your big chance. Are you prepared to do that?"

"Yes," Betty Marie said fervently. The simple word held conviction, and Mr. Denham sensed it.

6. "I Will Be Maria Tallchief"

The company's fall season in New York began almost at once. Betty Marie came to the theater early on opening night. She liked the controlled excitement in the air, the feeling of "tuning up," as if she were an instrument to be played. What part would she dance? she wondered. She was prepared for several, but corps girls never knew until the last moment.

Yazvinsky, the ballet master, touched her on the shoulder. "Get made up for the cancan in *Gaîté Parisienne.*"

Betty Marie was pleased. The cancan in the café scene was done by an ensemble of corps girls, and was fun to do. She rushed into the dressing room. The girls were chattering in front of the mirrors, putting on makeup, smoothing their sleek hair, diving into costumes. Madame Pourmel, the wardrobe mistress, was everywhere at once, holding out tutus, tightening a ribbon here, fastening a hook there, hunting shoes, placing a wreath in a girl's hair.

Betty Marie wriggled into her costume, ran her hands over her long hose, and applied the garish makeup for the cancan number.

A quick look in the mirror assured her that all was right. The dressing room was noisy. She went out and stood in the wings, shivering a little in the cold air that blew around her. Soon the musicians would come, the electricians would try out the lights. Then the hall would fill with women in lovely gowns and men in opera hats and white ties. There would be the rustle of programs and the subdued sound of many people talking.

Yazvinsky appeared out of nowhere. "Quick!"

he said. "Get out of that costume and get made up for the Lady in Green."

"But the cancan—"

"Forget it," he said curtly. "You've just got time. The *soliste* who's the Lady hasn't turned up. We can't wait for her. You know the part. Make up for it and use the rest of the time for rehearsing, if you need to."

Betty Marie, breathless over her good fortune, tore back to the dressing room. "I'm to be the Lady in Green!" she said to Madame Pourmel.

Without turning, Madame said, "Over there— the green costume in the closet. Try it on. I may have to take it in a little."

This was nothing new, apparently, to Madame Pourmel, but to Betty Marie it was exhilarating. Oh, she knew the part—but it might be a good idea to run through the steps.

She put on the new costume. The makeup would have to be changed, too. Madame said, "Here, let me help you."

Expertly she outlined Betty Marie's eyes and applied cream and powder. "You'll do," she said at last. "Run out, away from this madhouse, and get calmed down before you go on."

Standing in the wings again, she heard the music of *Gaîté Parisienne* in her head. Mentally, she went through the steps and the motions of the Lady in Green.

Suddenly she felt a tickle in her nose. Heavens, she needed a tissue. She ran to the dressing room. Pausing a moment in the doorway, she heard one of the corps girls saying loudly, "Fancies herself, doesn't she? Maybe she has hallucinations—taking all the parts herself tonight!"

Betty Marie, her face impassive, advanced to the table and snatched up a tissue. The girl who had made the remark turned her back; the others fell silent. Their envy and resentment was still hard to take, but Betty Marie had learned to let some of it slide by.

She was just about to leave when the *soliste* burst into the room. Her face was pink from rushing. "That dreadful subway! I thought I'd never get here. Madame, my costume—I just have time to get into it—"

Swiftly Betty Marie took off the costume of the Lady in Green and gave it to the woman to whom it belonged.

"Well, it was a short dream, wasn't it?" the girl at the table remarked. Betty Marie's dark eyes flashed; she said nothing. It *had* been a short dream.

She got back into her cancan costume. The callboy announced, "Five minutes to curtain time!" The lights went down, and *Gaîté Parisienne* went

Betty Marie, second row left, dances the cancan with the *Gaîté Parisienne* ensemble.

on. Betty Marie danced in the ensemble, lifting her long legs in *fouettés*, and feeling, even here, the envious glances of her corps mates. Yazvinsky and Madame and Slavenska had all praised her *fouettés*, the whipping motion of her legs while on her toes. It was one of the things she did extremely well. But the moment was swiftly over. She ran into the wings with the others.

Yazvinsky and Madame Pourmel grabbed her at once. "Quick, quick!" Yazvinsky said. Madame held out a costume. A hurried look and Betty Marie realized it was for an ensemble. "Drop your cancan costume," Madame ordered. She slipped the other dress over her head. "There's your cue!" Yazvinsky whispered loudly. His face was flushed and his hair was tousled.

Betty Marie ran back on stage with the girls of the ensemble. Somebody obviously was ill or had not showed up. The rehearsals, so endless and so constant, stood her in good stead. She went through the right motions, took her part in the group, and was again swept out into the wings while applause stirred through the house.

At the party following the performance, Mia Slavenska took her hand. "You did well," she said. "I was watching you."

"I think I could dance all the parts of *Gaîté* now in my sleep!" Betty Marie laughed.

Mia's face was serious. "Have you thought of a new name for yourself?" she asked. "A Russian one? You know Mr. Denham wants that; he spoke to me about it again today."

Betty Marie shook her head. "Why should I change my name? Helen hasn't and Freddie Franklin hasn't changed his, either."

"Helen is not Betty Marie," Slavenska said firmly. "Franklin is an individualist and a top performer. He can afford to take that stand."

"But I don't want to change my name."

"Think of something more flowing," Slavenska said. "Betty Marie makes one think of a little girl. It is not the name for one who may become a great dancer." She wrinkled her brow. "How about Lisa, for instance? Or Maria?"

Betty Marie said thoughtfully. "Just so it isn't Bettina! I couldn't stand that."

"We will ask the others," Slavenska said purposefully. She called them around her. "We must think of a name for the little one."

Someone said, "How about Tallchieva? What luck to have your real name turn into something Russian as easily as that!"

Betty Marie lifted her chin. "I will not change my last name," she said, her voice quiet. "I like it. I'm proud of it."

They argued with her. Even Mr. Denham tried to persuade her. "No, I won't change it. But my first name—that's something else. Maria goes well with Tallchief, and it's not a 'little girl' name. I will be known as Maria Tallchief."

George Denham's eyes narrowed. There was a stubborn streak in this young woman, but somehow he liked it. "Maria Tallchief," he repeated. "Maybe we can build on that. The Osage Indian dancer. It's different."

7. "You Won't Be Needed After All"

As she approached the Metropolitan Opera House, Maria Tallchief felt her pulse quicken. It was a homely building of red brick darkened by the city's grime, but it stood there, huge and sturdy and somehow romantic. She entered the side door. From the studios above came the subdued sounds of soaring soprano voices, the trill of a flute, the arpeggios on a piano. How many young hopefuls this old opera house held! And on its stage some of the most thrilling operas and dances in the world had been performed.

Maria smiled a little ruefully to herself. Those stage "boards" might do very well for singers, but they were dreadful for dancers—rough and dirty and full of hidden cracks that could trip you.

All kinds of things could trip you, she thought now, making her way to the wings. She had just come from the studio where the list of names had been posted for *Chopin Concerto*. Madame Nijinska had come east to rehearse it for its first professional performance. Surely, surely, her name would be on the list! But it wasn't. She tried to tell herself that she really hadn't expected it. Although she had danced in the ballet in Los Angeles, it had been an amateur production. And it was not even six months since she had come to New York. Just the same, her heart seemed to plummet to her shoes. It was a bitter disappointment that Madame hadn't remembered her pupil, Maria Tallchief, and given her a little part in it somewhere!

Rehearsal for *Rodeo* was in full swing. Agnes de Mille, the famous dancer and choreographer, was putting it on for Ballet Russe. Watching it, Maria almost forgot her heartache. What a stunning ballet it was! Completely American in setting, pace, and direction, it was quite an innovation for the Ballet Russe. Some of the dancers were horrified with the new ballet.

"It doesn't fit our repertoire," they said. "It's horse opera!"

But Maria liked it. She had wondered how some of the dancers would adjust to the new kind of choreography, so different from the classic ballet steps. She wondered particularly about Franklin, the *premier danseur*, who had been cast in the role of the Champion Roper. He was perfect, Maria thought rapturously, absolutely perfect, and she loved the way he leaped and stomped and bounded, as if he thoroughly enjoyed the part. Agnes de Mille herself was playing the part of the Cowgirl.

Lost in her thoughts, Maria was startled to feel a hand on her shoulder. She turned to look into the face of Agnes de Mille herself. "Go and get fitted for a costume," she said. "I've been watching you, and I've written in a little part for you."

It was unheard of! The choreographer had chosen her ahead of the other girls who had been there much longer! This didn't help to make Maria popular, but she was elated at her chance.

Rodeo was performed for the first time in October. Maria's part lasted only a minute or two. She whirled her skirts and flirted with Franklin, the Champion Roper. He ran after her, and the public loved it. Miss de Mille said that Maria "brought a quality of feeling" to her part.

Rodeo was an outstanding success. "You're on for the season," Miss de Mille told Maria. "I think I'll have Franklin start doing lifts for you."

To be lifted in the strong arms of the *premier danseur* and shown to the audience was honor indeed! "I just hope I don't do something silly," Maria said worriedly to Helen Kramer, "—or hit him in the eye! I did that to Lichine one day and he was furious!"

"Don't worry, Ducky," Franklin said, grinning, when he heard about it. "I won't let anything happen." As a matter of fact, he proved to be a perfect partner for their brief moments together.

The part in *Rodeo* was a small success for Maria, and helped to ease her pain at not having a part in *Chopin Concerto*. Somehow, that still mattered more than anything else in the world.

Maria continued to dance in *Rodeo* and other ballets in the repertoire, but she felt continually depressed and could not eat well. Tanya understood and offered her wordless sympathy. It got to be an obsession with Maria. She wanted to be in the *Concerto* above everything else.

She was watching the glamorous Krassovska rehearse the lead one day when Nijinska came up to her. The lead was the same role Maria had danced in the Hollywood Bowl, but it had been changed, as many of the parts had been, for Nijinska had rearranged them. "Watch her," Madame said now, "and the others, too." Those were the parts Cyd Charisse and Marjorie had taken. "You see how the parts have changed? Learn them. It would be well."

Maria wanted to cry out, "What's the use? I will never get the chance to do any of them." Her face felt frozen in mutinous lines.

Betty Marie hoped to follow in the footsteps of well-known stars of the Ballet Russe like Krassovska, above, and Danilova, seen here with Frederic Franklin.

As if she read her thoughts, Madame said calmly, "You must watch everyone, you must learn everything, so that when the time comes, you will be ready."

Oh, that was good advice, no doubt, but would her time ever come?

A few days later Yazvinsky said abruptly, "I want you to understudy the *solistes*."

The *solistes* were not pleased that Maria was studying them, preparing to take their places if they should fail, or become ill. Maria was sensitive to the chilly atmosphere, but it did not keep her from working harder than ever. When the time came—*if* the time came—she would be ready.

When *Chopin Concerto* opened at the Metropolitan Opera, Maria was in the wings. It was a triumphant opening: Danilova was superb as the prima ballerina, and Maria was worshipful. She watched Slavenska and Krassovska in the parts that she and Cyd Charisse had danced several years ago. Maria wrote home to her family, "I know I am stupid to care so much, but I feel terrible that I cannot dance in Nijinska's ballet."

As often as she could, she practiced by herself. She took lessons paid for with money that still came regularly from home. There were lessons from the company's *maître*, and lessons at the School of American Ballet. Sometimes she wondered why the other girls in the corps didn't prepare themselves as she was doing. Perhaps they didn't have the money, she thought.

The truth of the matter, she discovered to her amazement, was that many of the girls did not care enough about ballet to practice regularly.

As the season progressed, some of the girls in the corps who had been most unfriendly to Maria left for one reason or another. They went to Hollywood, married, or just dropped out, tired of working hard and getting nowhere. Maria was happy that Helen Kramer and her friends Ruth Rickman and Gertie Swobodina were still there.

Slavenska, too, was still her friend. "Come on stage with me," she told Maria often, "and dance behind me while I rehearse." This was a wonderful opportunity to study the dancer's style and control, and Maria made use of every chance.

"Heavens," one of the girls said, "Maria's a glutton for work! She understudies everybody— even the understudies!"

In late fall they began an American tour. Maria warned her family not to expect to see her in any featured part when they performed in Los Angeles. She wrote to her mother from San Francisco, "Here we are in Ruthie's home town, and she has been with the company for months and months, but she has not one special little thing to dance. If I were given something special in Los Angeles, it wouldn't be fair to the others."

She did have something to show her family, however, and that was a new friend. Sasha, a handsome young Russian dancer, had joined the Ballet Russe and was a company pet. The son of a Russian nobleman who had been a friend of the famous dancer Pavlova, Sasha could tell endless tales about the Imperial Russian Ballet. Maria listened with fascination, and soon Sasha singled her out for his attention. Members of the company looked on approvingly. Little Tallchief was keeping Sasha in line, they thought. Meanwhile, it was pleasant for Maria to have an admirer with whom she could practice her French!

The family in Beverly Hills liked Sasha immensely. He was a gentleman and he was delightful. They were glad that Maria had him as a friend.

By Christmas the company was back in New York. "Imagine it! Opening night on Christmas Day!" the girls moaned. They thought it was dreadful, an imposition. But it seemed thrilling to Maria. This would certainly be a Christmas to remember.

She opened her gifts Christmas morning with the happiness of a child. Such lovely gifts! Imported bath soaps and powder and cologne from some of the corps. Fleece-lined gloves from Ruth and a wooly bed jacket from Helen. They had teased her so often about how cold she had been in Canada.

When she opened the box from Sasha she let out a gasp of amazement and dismay. A ring with two rubies! Oh, it was beautiful! But how could she accept it? It was much too expensive.

She wrote home at once for advice. Her family must tell her quickly, quickly, what she should do. Should she return it? She yearned over it a long time and then put the ring back in its box.

She went to the theater and worked by herself for an hour before reporting for a class with Yazvinsky. He was talking to Mr. Denham, and she walked off to a corner to do some warming-up exercises. Yazvinsky left to call the class to order and Mr. Denham came up to her.

"Do you know the *Concerto* well?"

Her heartbeat quickened. "Yes," she replied without hesitation.

"There's a possibility you may have a role in it tomorrow night," he said. Maria could hardly believe her ears. "You had better stay after the performance tonight and have a workout with Slavenska. Tomorrow you will have to practice the changes that have been made."

Maria went through the class in a daze.

After class Helen said, "What in the world did Denham say to you? You looked as if he'd turned you into a princess with his fairy wand."

Maria told her, and Helen stared back in amazement, glad for her friend's good fortune. "Come to dinner," she urged now. "You'll need it!"

"I couldn't eat a bite," Maria said. "Not a bite."

Helen insisted, "You have to eat something!"

Maria looked with distaste at the menu. "Turkey ... pumpkin pie ... I'd choke on it," she said. "I'll just have a cup of chocolate."

Mia Slavenska was at the restaurant with a party of friends. She stopped to say to Maria, "Good news, little one!"

"Oh, I can hardly believe it! But Mr. Denham didn't say *which* role I would dance."

"I can tell you that. It is Krassovska's."

The impact of her words was tremendous. Krassovska's role! "I know the whole thing," Maria said happily, "except for some parts of the *vivace*."

"We will work together after the performance tonight," Slavenska said. "I will help you. But there will be no music, you know."

"I can dance it without music," Maria said gaily. "I know every note."

The news of Maria's luck spread at the theater, and her friends were warm in their good wishes. They gathered together in the wings to watch the premiere. Maria felt as if she were in a dream. It couldn't be true! Krassovska's role! Krassovska was temperamental; she had been difficult lately. Perhaps she had said she would not dance unless she received more money.

It was almost curtain time. A corps girl came and touched Maria on the shoulder. "Danilova wants to see you," she announced curtly.

"Danilova herself?" It was like being summoned before a five-star general. She hurried to the dressing room.

Mr. Denham was there, too. Danilova, exquisite and cool, said gently, "Have you ever danced in *Concerto*?"

"Oh, yes," Maria said quickly. "I danced one of the lead roles—your role, Madame—at the Hollywood Bowl."

Danilova turned to Denham and said something in Russian. Maria waited eagerly. Mr. Denham said, "Madame thinks it would be a pity for you to dance in *Concerto* without proper rehearsal. She thinks it would not be possible for a dancer to learn this long, difficult role by tomorrow."

"Oh," Maria said, clasping her hands, "I am sure I could! I will try. I know the movements, I know the music, so well!"

Early next day she was at the theater, practicing. Of course she could do it! Nijinska had told her to watch everything, to watch everybody, to practice all roles, so that when the time came she would be ready. "I am sure I am ready," she said to herself with confidence. How proud Nijinska would be of her now!

Just the same, she was glad to see Mia Slavenska appear. "We will rehearse together," Mia said. "I will take Krassovska's part and you must follow everything I do."

The day sped by in furious preparation. Toward evening the tension mounted. The corps girls clustered around her, some frankly envious, some exclaiming happily over her good fortune. Helen insisted on fussing with Maria's hair and costume, and Ruth wanted to tie her ballet slippers. "No,"

Maria said seriously, "that I want to do myself. They have to be just right for me, you know."

"You're a modern Cinderella," Helen said fondly. "Understudy goes on in starring role! I can just see the headlines!"

Maria was ready early and went to stand in the wings. Mr. Denham came up to her. "You won't be needed, after all," he said brusquely.

Maria could only look the question that beat in her mind. Why, why?

"Krassovska's role will be taken by Slavenska," he said, and moved on.

It was a cruel, bitter blow. She went backstage, took off her costume, and changed into street clothes. She returned to the apartment to wait for Helen. She wasn't hungry and could only swallow a glass of milk. Instead of eating she wrote again to her family, telling them of the incredible turn of events, trying to work out on paper the puzzle of this whole thing.

There must be a reason, there must be! Perhaps Danilova hadn't wanted to dance with her, and that's why Mr. Denham had not let her go on. How else could she explain it? Yet she mustn't worry them at home too much. She told them she was tired, and she ended, "It's cold and I've had a long day."

What a strange series of events this had been!

8. "Fatten Yourself Up!"

For the next few days Maria Tallchief was the talk of the ballet world. Rumors flew around like dandelion fluff—and with just as much substance to them. Maria heard many of the rumors at one time or another... Krassovska had refused to continue with the company until she had been given the salary she was asking for; Danilova refused to dance with the young American because she was better *en pointe* than Danilova herself; Danilova did not want to appear in a ballet in which the other main role was taken by a mere corps girl.

The girls in the corps were divided in their loyalties. Some sympathized strongly with Tallchief; others were in Danilova's camp. Maria tried hard to remain calm and not to be too hurt by all the rumors circling around her.

During the New Year holidays, Danilova gave a party and invited Maria and Sasha to it. Sasha was still Maria's friend, although she had returned his costly ring. During the evening Danilova drew Maria aside.

"I know you have been wondering why you did not appear in *Chopin Concerto*," she said. She spoke English with a delightful accent.

Maria nodded. The hurt was still there and words stuck in her throat.

"Perhaps you hate me," Danilova said. "I could understand that. But, truly, you would never have forgiven yourself if you had danced the part and not done well. There was not enough time for you to be ready for it."

Maria thought rebelliously, I *could* have done it, I know I could. But, wisely, she said nothing.

The ballerina pulled her down beside her on a

couch. "I have spoken to Yazvinsky," she said. "There is a role, a small one, in *Le Beau Danube* [The Beautiful Danube]. I have been watching you and I think you may do very well in it."

Maria was grateful, but still the pain persisted. She had not yet been able to prove herself—to Danilova, to Yazvinsky, to anyone.

Doggedly, however, she kept on with classes. That winter was a rugged one. A virus struck the company and downed one member after another. Two *solistes* went to the hospital. Ruth, Maria's roommate, caught a cold which later turned into pneumonia. Understudies were rehearsed madly and put into various roles.

Maria caught a cold, too. She could not seem to get rid of it. When she was given a part in *Schéhérazade* as a sultan's wife, it did not lift her spirits. She was supposed to writhe and slink along the floor in a "sexy" way which seemed silly to her. "At least," she told Sasha, "I've learned to wrap a turban!"

Mrs. Tallchief wrote that she was worried about Maria's health and that she did not seem to be

Maria Tallchief dancing in *Ballet Imperial*, one of her early roles for the Ballet Russe.

making progress with the company. Marjorie was studying under Nijinska, who had returned to Hollywood. Why couldn't Maria come back and study with her, too? It would be much better, her mother thought, to be at home.

But Maria's stubborn determination came to the fore. She replied that she was learning a great deal at Ballet Russe and that the touring experience was invaluable. Besides, she added, now that the company was depleted by illness, she certainly must stay on and help out in any way she could.

In April the Ballet Russe went on tour once more, starting in Pittsburgh. Danilova held classes daily, followed by rehearsals. The weather was chilly and the air was heavy. One girl after another caught a cold or fainted in class. Finally Maria, too, became ill. Although a constant low fever and aching limbs made her miserable, she continued to dance. At night, she rubbed her chest with liniment and tried to forget her aches and pains. Not long ago Maria had worried about being too fat. Now she worried about losing so much weight.

Mrs. Tallchief wrote Maria that Marjorie had been invited to join the Los Angeles Light Opera Company. This would be a wonderful opportunity for Maria to come home—she could dance there, too. But Maria held steadfast. She was under contract and she could not possibly leave the Ballet Russe. She obediently took her cough medicine, as Mia reminded her to do, and swallowed quinine pills to try to get rid of her fever.

One night while dancing at a private party, Maria fainted and fell to the floor. Her hosts were most concerned. The next day she found a case of soup waiting for her at the apartment. They had heard, they said, what a difficult life dancers led. Wouldn't she please use this to build herself up again?

Sasha whooped with laughter when he heard about it. "In Russia in the old days admirers sent dancers beautiful bouquets with diamonds or rubies hidden in them. And here they send soup! What a country!"

Maria laughed over it, too, but she said she appreciated the gift because of its thoughtfulness.

Between performances, Maria practiced and practiced, even when she was not feeling well. She worked especially hard rehearsing the various *Concerto* roles, and Danilova herself helped her. When Danilova praised her work, Maria's spirits soared.

May 1, 1943 was a day Maria would never forget. "Krassovska has hurt her foot," Yazvinsky told her. "She will not be dancing in *Concerto*. Go to Madame Pourmel and get outfitted for the matinee."

At last, at last! This time, surely, she would be able to go on! The girls helped Maria dress.

"Here," Helen said, "is a good luck charm. Make it work!" And Sasha said dramatically, "I am so excited I shall lose my lunch!"

When Maria's cue came, she leaped onstage. She danced as she had never danced before, but she did not know it. She felt nothing, knew nothing, until she was back in the wings. It was as if the whole thing had been a dream. All she knew was that she had not fallen on stage!

Mia was waiting for her. "You did wonderfully!

I'm proud of you." Then Danilova came up to her. "I want to congratulate you," the prima said. "I liked your dancing very, very much."

It was a proud moment. Best of all, perhaps, were Mia's words as she accompanied Maria to the dressing room. Mia told her that the ballet master thought she was the only girl in the corps who looked as if she would become a real ballerina. Maria hugged that precious pronouncement.

Freddie Franklin burst into the dressing room as she was getting ready for the street. He took both her hands. "Ducky, you were marvelous! You're a wonderfully dramatic dancer!"

Mr. Denham came by, too. "You did well, Tallchief," he said in his matter-of-fact way. "You'll dance Krassovska's role till she is well again."

Maria knew that this was only a temporary triumph, but she savored it while she could. As the tour continued Krassovska danced certain roles, but not in *Concerto*, because it required too much work *en pointe*.

"It's too bad," Helen said indignantly, "that

they haven't changed the printed programs. Krassovska's name is still on it, yet you're dancing the role."

Maria smiled. "I don't mind too much," she said. The audience might not be aware of who was taking the part, but the people who mattered *did* know—Mia and Danilova and Yazvinsky. They knew; therefore she could wait.

Maria had hoped to go home for a visit when the tour ended. But instead of a summer vacation, the girls got word that Ballet Russe would play a summer season, and rehearsals would start within a week.

Krassovska was better now and she would dance in *Concerto* in New York. But two ballets were being revived, *Coppélia* and *Igrouchky*, and Maria would have small parts in both, as well as in *Le Beau Danube*. That was good enough for the present.

Then Mr. Denham called her into his office. "Krassovska has decided to go to Europe," he said suddenly. "She will be leaving the company. You will take her role in *Concerto* permanently."

While Maria stood silently before him, trying to ease her excited breathing, he said, "You look terrible! What's the matter with you? You've lost weight. Your eyes look sunken. Fatten yourself up—drink milk, eat steaks!"

It was an order. She nodded wordlessly. Happiness overwhelmed her. At last she would be able to prove herself to New York critics in the role that meant so much to her.

Maria wrote home in great haste, asking Marjorie to send her some of her toe slippers. "I can't get any made in time," she said, "and I'm afraid the ones I have will fall apart." Marjorie promptly sent her several pairs. "Good luck when you wear them!" she said.

Eighteen-year-old Maria's New York debut in *Concerto* was a great success. Members of the company crowded around her backstage, congratulating her. The corps girls had sent her an enormous bunch of roses, and to Maria this was especially touching. After the debut, there was a big party at the St. Regis Hotel, and then Madame Danilova had another at the Casino Russe.

It was a deliriously joyful time. But the next day at the rehearsal for *Le Beau Danube*, she was just a corps girl again—and content to be one. Although Maria was dancing a lead role in *Concerto*, she would continue to dance in the corps in other ballets to be presented during the season.

Still, her name was now on the program, and she had an opportunity to dance her *Concerto* role several times during the next few weeks. The publicity department saw a golden chance. "The beautiful dancing Osage! Come on now, give us some romantic or glamorous stories about yourself to use as newspaper material!"

Maria looked nonplussed. "But I haven't anything like that to tell you!" she protested.

At the close of the summer season Denham offered her a two-year contract. "I'll have to talk it over with my parents," she said slowly.

He wasn't a bit pleased. "Talk it over, then, and let me know. Not every girl gets a chance like this."

She went home to California full of plans. Maybe she could persuade Marjorie to join the

Ballet Russe, too, and to share an apartment with her in New York. Marjorie had graduated from high school, but she had no desire to leave home. Life was very pleasant where she was. She was surrounded by boyfriends, and she had had a part in a movie, dancing with the Lichines.

In spite of Maria's pleadings, Mrs. Tallchief would not let her sign the contract. She criticized the company for making Betty Marie wait so long to get a role in *Concerto*.

"They haven't made any definite promises about future roles," her mother said. "You don't want to tie yourself down for two years." She wrote Mr. Denham that she would allow her daughter to return to the Ballet Russe only if there were no contract.

Mr. Denham replied posthaste that he could hardly give a dancer important roles if he had no way of knowing how long she would be part of the company.

But Mrs. Tallchief was disturbed. Friends had told her that Krassovska was rejoining the company. If she did, there would be fewer chances for Maria. Also there was to be a new choreographer and ballet master.

"Who?" Maria asked curiously.

"George Balanchine."

"Really!" Maria said in excitement. "He's wonderful! The things he has presented are absolutely stunning. He'll put new life into the Ballet Russe."

"But he has his own protégés," said Mrs. Tallchief. "He'll probably bring many of them with him. If you return to the company, it must be without a contract."

So Maria went back to New York. She was sure of nothing except that she would be dancing again, and dancing was as necessary to her as breathing.

9. "One Learns to Stand Alone"

Standing disconsolately in front of the bulletin board, Maria knew that difficulties were ahead of her. Her mother was right—Krassovska's name was there, and so were quite a few new names, all American. One of them she recognized—Yvonne Chouteau. That was the half-Indian girl who had been in one of Mr. Belcher's classes in Los Angeles.

The girls of the corps had plenty to tell her. "Denham's down on you because you wouldn't sign up."

"Wait till Balanchine gets here! They say he has his own favorites, and we won't have a chance —you, either!"

One of the new dancers, Mary Ellen Moylan, a Balanchine protégée, was featured almost at once. That sort of thing hurt. Quite seriously Maria studied Moylan's dancing. "I know I'm better," she said to herself. "I have more fire."

Nijinska came back to Ballet Russe to put on one of her own ballets, *Étude*, and Maria was given a part in it. That buoyed her spirits, and it was good to be working with Madame again. The company went on tour and *Étude* was first performed in Cleveland. Maria, though she kept it to herself, did not care for the ballet. It seemed artificial and stylized. She felt almost relieved when the audiences did not care for it, either. They could not understand it, and preferred the other ballets that the company did.

Maria felt sorry for Nijinska, but Madame shrugged. "One must be philosophical about these things," she said. "People abroad loved it."

The worst of it was that Ballet Russe was getting poor press reviews. More and more the critics compared Ballet Russe with its rival, Ballet Theatre, unfavorably. The American company was putting on new, dynamic dances with modern American plots and dramatic scenes, and with more and more American dancers. The Ballet Russe usually limited itself to classical ballet.

As soon as Maria's company returned to New York, she hurried to see some of the Ballet Theatre productions, and she came away full of admiration. No wonder they were getting rave reviews! She began to wonder ... should she stay with Ballet Russe? The company had few American *solistes*, and only one had ever been billed as a prima—a star. What chance did she have?

When the company's new souvenir program came out, however, she felt better. Photographs of the more important dancers were in the front part of the program. There she was at last! She thought it was a silly pose that had been chosen —with a finger under her chin. But at least she was there, listed as a *soliste*! She giggled over the names Elena Kramarr and Ruth Riekman—her old friends, Helen Kramer and Ruth Rickman. Ruthie was going to marry a musician in the orchestra, and everyone thought it very romantic.

Then Maria got a piece of news that sent her spirits plunging again. "I am leaving Ballet Russe," Mia told her. "I am starting a school of my own."

"But you can't leave!" Maria cried. "You've been such a wonderful friend, such wonderful help. I'll feel lost without you."

Mia was touched, but she said firmly, "One learns to stand alone. And we can still be friends, can we not?"

"Always," Maria said fervently. But Mia had been her teacher, her comforter, her mentor. It would be hard not to have her there.

One of the girls said pertly, "Don't feel too bad! If Slavenska isn't with us any more, maybe you'll be chosen to dance the roles she was featured in. Didn't you ever think of that?"

Maria hardly wanted to think of it. But, yes, it was a possibility. Hadn't she studied with Slavenska, danced behind her, and been coached by her?

Balanchine took over active direction of Ballet Russe in the spring of 1944. At the same time he was choreographing *Song of Norway* for Broadway production. It was a musical based on the life of the composer Edvard Grieg, and ballet was only a part of it, but an important part. Everyone wondered whom he would choose from the Ballet Russe to dance in it. Franklin, of course, they agreed on. "And Danilova, no doubt! After all, she's a prima and he was once married to her!"

Danilova it was. Balanchine watched all the dancers at Ballet Russe. "You," he said one day to Maria, "will understudy Danilova."

It seemed an incredible piece of luck. When Maria went home for a quick visit, she talked things over with Marjorie. "You must come to New York now," she said. "The Ballet Russe is so exciting with Balanchine running it. You must join."

"I *am* coming to New York," Marjorie said. "I'm joining Ballet Theatre with the Lichines. David is choreographing *Graduation Ball*, and there's a part in it for me. I'm going to *fouetté* to my heart's content!"

Maria said almost wistfully, "How easily things

come your way! It must be your temperament. You're gay and life's entrancing. I'm the serious one. But, oh, I'm so glad for you!"

They still looked like twins, as everyone said, but now the difference in temperament and approach to life was more marked. "Little sister" had grown up, Maria discovered, and was able to be a success on her own.

Song of Norway opened in August and captured the New York audiences at once. Danilova was electric in her role, and Danilova fan clubs sprang up everywhere. Maria thought the prima ballerina was ravishing.

The musical was such a success that its season was extended, yet it was time for Ballet Russe to begin its own fall performances. The ballet company needed its star attraction, Danilova. Balanchine, who had seen Maria's work as understudy, suggested to the producer that she step into Danilova's part.

Maria was stunned. "I must think about it," she begged. It would mean star billing, more money, and it might lead to even greater things—

The curtain is about to go up! In the wings the wardrobe mistress repairs Maria's costume.

"But, no, I must refuse," she decided finally. "I want to stay in legitimate ballet." It was a decision most of the company could not understand. She was turning down a chance for fame and riches. But Balanchine was pleased. He saw her now as someone he could use in bigger and better roles, someone he could build up as he had built up other ballerinas.

Balanchine was known for his absolute mastery of the corps and the principals in his ballets. He thought out even the slightest movement, and showed his dancers just how he wanted everything done. He was gentle and patient, but he never stopped coaching them until he had exactly the effect and precisely the movement that he had in mind. Some of the dancers rebelled at his methods—"He makes a puppet of you," they said —but Maria responded to his direction and worked tirelessly for him.

Balanchine had a genius for inspiring his dancers and for giving new life to some of the older ballets. Under his guidance they emerged fresh and unusual, as if they had just been invented. His was the "Balanchine touch," and his direction gave the Ballet Russe new vigor. It was a keen competitor now of the Ballet Theatre.

Audiences in New York City enjoyed both companies. Some avid ballet lovers would go to the first half of one performance, then rush in taxis to see the second half of the other performance.

On nights when she wasn't performing, Maria went to the Ballet Theatre to watch. It so happened that she never had a chance to see her sister dance, but she did manage to see her beloved

Tanya, Lichine's wife. Tanya was at the height of her career. "Oh, she is simply beautiful!" Maria sighed. "She floats through the air!" Audiences adored her, and Maria knew that Tanya and Danilova were constant inspirations for her.

Working with Balanchine was of invaluable help to Maria. She felt herself developing, changing, and becoming more and more the kind of dancer she wished to become. But when she was interviewed and asked to give advice for young beginning dancers she said, "How could I give advice? I myself am still learning."

Many of the important roles went to Mary Ellen Moylan, but finally Maria was rewarded for her patience and skill. Balanchine had created a ballet, *Ballet Imperial*, to the music of Tchaikovsky's Piano Concerto no. 2. This was music from her student days that she knew as well as Chopin's Concerto, and she was happy when she was given a part. She was sure she could dance it beautifully. Maybe she tried too hard, for Moylan received ecstatic notices in the press, and Maria was dismissed in a line or two.

It was a blow to her. But Balanchine did not let her remain downhearted for long. He decided to let her dance to the dreamy *valse* music of Chopin in *Les Sylphides*. How long ago it seemed that she had watched Tanya perform that charming, graceful "Waltz Variation!" And now she was to have her own opportunity. She let her love of the music and of the ballet shine through her movements, and the critics raved about her. They even wondered if she would ever be able to repeat that rapturous performance.

The public had become aware of Maria Tallchief. They were almost equally aware of Marjorie Tallchief. It was amazing to have two sisters performing in the two main ballet companies at the same time in New York. Marjorie took her popularity lightly, as she did all things. To Maria it was a serious business. She practiced endlessly, took good care of her long legs, kept her back straight, her head high, and followed a rigid regime.

More and more Balanchine used Maria in important roles.

"Why not?" some of the jealous company members said. "She does everything just the way he wants it."

But others saw things in a different light. "She deserves the roles," they said, "and they work so well together."

That was true, as Maria and Balanchine soon realized. They were both deeply musical, and when he had a definite idea of what the score could mean and how it should be interpreted, Maria could feel it with him. Occasionally they went out to dinner together, relishing their mutual interest in music and the dance. At rehearsals Balanchine devoted particular attention to her roles.

The corps members began to gossip. "He's more than interested in her," they said. The gossip grew more persistent when Balanchine and his wife, Vera Zorina, the dancer, were divorced early in 1946.

10. "A Contract Is a Promise"

Balanchine called Maria to him one day. His short frame and balding head contrasted with her long legs and sleek black hair caught back against her neck. His voice was soft. "I am putting on *Le Baiser de la Fée* [The Fairy's Kiss]," he said. "You know the story of the Ice Maiden that Hans Christian Andersen wrote."

"Oh, yes." She remembered, too, that Slavenska had danced it six years ago.

"You will be the Fairy," Balanchine said calmly. Maria was overcome. That was Slavenska's role, the one that required the dancer to be first the Ice Maiden, then the gypsy fortune-teller, then the beautiful bride—without letting the audience forget that she was also the Fairy. Slavenska had told her how difficult the role was.

"I am not asking you if you can do it," Balanchine's soft voice went on. "I know you can, if you do as I say. We start rehearsals at once."

Maria felt the honor deeply. She also felt the responsibility, for Balanchine had brought the Ballet Russe to new prominence with his brilliant presentations and his new ideas. This ballet would be one of the most important of the new season. She must not fail him—or herself.

The Fairy that he evolved for Maria was quite different from Slavenska's. It was designed to show Maria's fluid grace and amazing skill.

On opening night the audience packed the New York City Center where the Ballet Russe was now performing. They were to see their favorites, Danilova and Freddie Franklin...and they were also to see a new Tallchief, a dancer they had never really seen before. They watched, amazed as she danced a graceful *pas de deux* with Franklin, whipped herself into a frenzy as the Gypsy,

and then became, before their very eyes, the regal and glacial Ice Maiden. It was an astounding performance and the audience went wild. The next morning the critics announced that a new ballerina had been born: "The beautiful dancing Osage."

Maria naturally felt happy over this exuberant praise. At the same time she couldn't help wondering if the critics and the audience would like her as well in the next ballet she was doing under Balanchine. In this, *Night Shadow*, she took the part of a coquette. The part was so different from anything she had ever done before that she felt unsure and a little frightened.

It was only ten days later that she went onstage as the coquette. At the end of the performance a full-throated cry rose from the audience—"Brava! Brava, Tallchief!"

The press kept calling her a ballerina—the equivalent of a star—but in the Ballet Russe this was a title not easily earned or lightly applied. Maria recognized this, even if some of the company members thought she was not getting her due.

Maria turned that aside. "I am learning a great deal under Balanchine," she said. His direction gave the company one of its most successful seasons. It came as a real shock when he told company members one day that he was leaving.

"I am starting a new ballet company," he said, "with my old friend Lincoln Kirstein. We're going to call it Ballet Society." The two men had founded the School of American Ballet, and now they wanted to work together again.

The company members could talk of nothing else. They wondered what would happen to Maria Tallchief. If Balanchine were gone, perhaps she wouldn't get so many of the plum roles.

They were even more amazed when, a month after Balanchine had left, they heard that he and Maria had married on August 16, 1946. Maria Tallchief was now Mrs. George Balanchine. "Why, he's almost twenty years older than she!" they cried.

The company members put their heads together. Tongues wagged. Now what would Maria do? She had a contract with Ballet Russe, but her husband would have a new company. Would she break her contract to dance under him? Everyone was sure that would be her decision.

But Maria said, "I wouldn't think of breaking my contract with Ballet Russe. A contract is a promise, and George agrees with me."

The year that followed was not an easy one for Maria. Because they knew that she would leave the company when her contract expired, the management and the ballet master did not give her interesting or important roles. With Balanchine gone they reverted to doing the same old ballets they had done for years.

The critics were quick to see the difference and said so. Maria could not help feeling that some of this was her fault, and she tried to dance even better than before. She tried so hard that she injured her foot and for a while she could not dance at all! The company fell into the doldrums until Danilova brought it to life again with an electrifying performance as the notorious British dancer, Lola Montez. Maria was more admiring of Danilova than ever.

Business picked up, and the critics were enthusiastic again when Ballet Russe put on *Ballet Imperial*, one of Balanchine's ballets. This time Maria was outstanding in it. The newspapers insisted on calling her an Indian princess, and the publicity department of Ballet Russe decided to play this up. In spite of Maria's protests that she was not an Indian princess, she began to be known as one, and audiences flocked to see her.

When the company went on tour, Maria was surrounded by admirers. They begged her for autographs, brought her flowers, and wrote her letters. They even sent her boxes of fig cookies because she had once said she liked them.

The management, recognizing her popularity, thought perhaps they should dignify her with the title, ballerina. She had earned it. As the end of her contract neared, they urged her to stay with Ballet Russe. What chance of continuing her popularity would she have with an untried group like Ballet Society, which performed for only a small list of subscribers? But at the end of her contract Maria left to be with George.

11. "You Do What You Have to Do"

George had gone to Paris on a temporary engagement as choreographer and ballet master for the Paris Opéra. Maria had always wanted to go to Paris and was looking forward to the trip for two reasons—it would be a kind of happy vacation, and she would see her sister. Marjorie was now a member of the Grand Ballet du Marquis de Cuevas and was in love with its *premier danseur*, George Skibine. What an exciting reunion it would be!

Maria had not expected to dance in Paris. But she found that Balanchine intended to put her on as the Fairy in *Le Baiser de la Fée*. Dance lovers in Paris were eager to see his guest dancer, Tamara Toumanova, whom they knew and loved. But who was this American dancer he had brought over? No American had danced in ballet at the Opéra for more than a hundred years! They were reluctant to welcome her. She was an upstart, a newcomer.

Balanchine enjoyed challenges. He felt sure that Maria would be as sensational in Paris as she had been in New York. Maria proved him right.

The audience responded as wildly as the New York audience had. Maria was the talk of Paris. English ballet fans flew from London to see her perform. Dancers spoke of her fantastic ability to move in any direction with ease. Critics praised her magic, her intensity, and her splendor, which they felt were due to her Indian background. The Opéra had never had a better season.

Maria was happy that Balanchine was proud of her. It was fun, too, to explore Paris with George, who knew it so well. Marjorie and Skibine often went with them.

After a performance, Maria and George would

return to their apartment. She would put her feet up while he cooked her a gourmet meal. He prided himself on his ability to cook, and he was also a good cabinetmaker, he told her. While they ate his delicious concoctions, they would discuss that evening's ballet, living it over again. It was a happy time.

But the season in Paris was a short one, and soon they were back in New York. George had to begin his season at Ballet Society. "As for you, Maria," he said, "I want you to go back to school."

Maria thought silently: After all that acclaim in Paris! He said, "Your technique is getting a little careless. You seem to have forgotten some of the basic things."

He must be right. He was always right. Uncomplainingly she went back to school. After a hard day's practice she and George would play duets on the grand piano in their apartment. They both relished music, but Maria would sigh, "If my teacher could hear me now! I'm so rusty!"

It wasn't long before Balanchine felt that Maria was more than ready to appear again, and he presented her in the ballet *Orpheus* with Tanaquil LeClercq. Tanaquil was a lovely red-haired girl with a high-strung temperament. She and Maria contrasted interestingly, for Maria, with her dark beauty, gave the impression of mystery and pride.

For her performance as Eurydice, Maria received the annual Dance Magazine Award for "memorable lyric quality, for command and growing compassion."

It was a well-deserved honor and Maria felt that now she could afford a real vacation. She and Balanchine went to Europe again.

"I am really thrilled," Maria told her friend Helen. "George has been commissioned to do the choreography for the Grand Ballet du Marquis de Cuevas."

It would be a wonderful chance to see Marjorie once more. Marjorie was now married to the dancer Skibine, whom she called Yura. The two recently married couples enjoyed a happy and relaxing summer.

The next season in New York, Balanchine and

The corps waits offstage for its cue as Maria
dances *en pointe* in the *Scotch Symphony*.

his company were installed in the City Center permanently. They had done extremely well the previous season, and from now on they would be known as the New York City Ballet Company.

Dance lovers expected miracles from Balanchine —new and exciting ballets. But Balanchine's moods changed. What he wanted to do that year were mostly plotless "mood" pieces. Business fell off and at the end of the first season in their new quarters company members left to take temporary jobs with other ballet companies. Maria became a guest performer with Ballet Theatre.

There she discovered that her partner would be Youskevitch. Youskevitch—her idol as a young girl!

She was nervous at first, but Youskevitch was not only a splendid dancer, he was also a considerate one. In the beginning their partnership was stiff and formal, but gradually they found the way to complement each other, and then their dancing was magical.

Meanwhile, Balanchine had a plan. "I am putting on *Firebird*," he told Maria, "for you."

Maria gasped. How could she be this supernatural creature, half bird, half woman, who would save the prince from the dreadful monsters in the forest? "I don't know if I can do it," she said hesitantly.

"You can," he retorted. "I will tell you every move. I will create it anew for you."

He had grown up with the Russian legend. He knew every note of the music Stravinsky had written for the story. Fokine had created a *Firebird* ballet years ago. It had been presented many times, but Balanchine's was a new and thrilling version. He had invented it for this amazing bird-woman who was his wife.

Maria did not want to fail him. She had only one week to prepare for the role—an almost superhuman task. But the part of the Firebird caught her in its challenge. She had to cover the stage in swift, bounding leaps, and her rapid turns and soaring movements had to make the audience believe she was a bird in flight—a bird of fire.

Balanchine presented the ballet with oriental splendor, sparing no expense to achieve the effect

Maria's portrayal of the Firebird reflected the un-
tamed spirit of this legendary bird-woman.

of richness and color that he wanted. November 27, 1949, Tallchief leaped onto the stage. Her body was encased in flaming red as if it were her skin; her arms and shoulders glittered with gold dust. A long red feather sprang from her head and quivered in the air as she moved.

She *was* the Firebird of legend and history. The audience drew in its breath and followed the leaping savage creature blazing across the stage. They knew that they were seeing the glorious performance of a true ballerina.

Balanchine had realized that the Firebird was the kind of creature Maria's Indian forebears might have worshiped long ago, and that Maria Tallchief would have the inner fire to portray it.

Critics and dancers praised Maria. They said "her tremendous technical ability, and her combination of ease and fire are the marvel of the era."

Reporters asked Maria how she could dance the *Firebird*. It seemed too full of difficulties for a human being to surmount. Maria had an answer.

"You do what you have to do," she said, "and when you must, you do a little more."

12. "Princess of Two Standards"

At the end of the New York season Maria left her husband for a temporary engagement with Ballet Theatre, which was playing in Chicago. She was to be prima ballerina there and could have her pick of roles.

Ballet Theatre had quite a few Balanchine ballets in its repertoire. They had not been popular with audiences in the Midwest, but with Tallchief interpreting them, the directors felt this would change. Tallchief would know how to present them!

Maria danced beautifully in her husband's ballets; she felt she had never done better. Even so, the audiences rejected them. They did not understand them. It was a bitter pill to swallow, and Tallchief returned to New York when the engagement was over, worried about her failure as a prima ballerina in Chicago.

She need not have worried. On opening night in New York she danced *Firebird* again. Her creation and her dancing were so stunning and beautiful that the audience sat in absolute silence for a moment after it ended. This was the supreme tribute. Then a storm of applause broke out, as people emerged from the spell she had cast.

Keyed up, nervous, and tense, Maria felt that she should rest. But she could not. Balanchine had more plans for her. He presented her as the Siren in his ballet, *The Prodigal Son.*

It was disastrous. Tallchief was not the audiences' idea of a siren. They did not respond to her in the role and Maria felt this keenly. It was her failure, not Balanchine's, she believed.

Balanchine said calmly, "We will try something else."

In July the New York City Ballet Company

went to England for a summer season at the Royal Opera House in London.

From the beginning things went wrong. The audiences did not care for the *Firebird*—they preferred Fokine's older version. Oddly enough, they liked *The Prodigal Son*, which New York had spurned! The company's dancers found themselves at a disadvantage on the huge stage of the Opera House for they were used to the smaller stages at home. They had to make all kinds of adjustments. Then on opening night Tallchief fell and hurt her right ankle.

"You must not go on," the house physician told her, but Maria found this unbearable. She *had* to go on! However, the pain became worse and worse. Finally she bowed out and Melissa Hayden finished the ballet. Later, Maria came down with a virus infection, and knew she was not doing her best. Then Melissa Hayden had an accident on stage. Stunned, she could barely crawl off into the wings.

Even with all the problems, the company was asked to extend its season, and, hoping for an upsurge in their fortunes, they agreed. But it was not a fortunate decision. They played to half-empty houses, and finally ended with a debt of over forty thousand dollars.

It was a saddened troupe that returned home. Maria was saddest of all. During their London engagement she and Balanchine had agreed that their marriage was not working out, and that it should be dissolved. They told the press that, although they would no longer be married, they would continue to work together in the ballet field.

Maria took her things from the New York apartment they had shared and went to live with her friend Vida Brown, who was Balanchine's assistant. Maria was now twenty-five years old.

When the autumn season opened, something happened to help cheer Maria. She had a new partner. André Eglevsky, a man of fine physique, had danced in every major ballet company and knew exactly how to show a prima ballerina's good points to best advantage. Youskevitch had done that for Tallchief, in a way, but Maria and Eglevsky were so well suited to each other that her dancing showed him up to best advantage as well. Together they were superb. The critics searched for new words to describe the thrill of seeing them dancing in perfect unison and understanding. One critic reported that sometimes, watching them, you felt such ecstacy that you could hardly bear it.

The "something else" that Balanchine had thought up for Maria was the part of the Swan Queen in *Swan Lake*. It is a part that every ballerina longs to do, a kind of supreme test of her quality as a dancer. With Eglevsky as her partner in the *pas de deux*, she was ravishing. She danced as if she were made of air and fire.

The following year Balanchine took his New York City Ballet Company abroad. In Zurich, Switzerland, where Maria and Eglevsky danced in *Swan Lake*, the audiences whistled and cheered, and Maria had to take fifteen curtain calls. In Holland the Dutch were charmed by her dancing and her beauty. During the adagio passage the audience let out its breath as one person in pure admiration.

From Amsterdam Maria rushed to Paris to see her new nephews. Marjorie had given birth to twin boys, and Maria was delighted with them. "Now I *will* have to perfect my French, so I can talk to them!" she vowed.

Everywhere the company went Maria had a personal triumph, but one which she shared with her partner. When she returned to the United States Maria found she was now in great demand, and she danced many roles. People began to think of her as the American prima ballerina, the first one. Wasn't she born in this country, of an Indian father and a Kansas mother? Hadn't her schooling and training been wholly American?

People in Oklahoma were especially proud of her. June 29, 1953 was declared Maria Tallchief Day. The Osage Tribal Council was proud of its daughter, too. She must return to Fairfax to be the guest of honor at a morning reception and then at an Indian dinner. There was squaw bread fried in deep fat, dried corn boiled with beef, and steamed beef.

Maria was thrilled to the bone. She was back

in her childhood, hearing stories of her Indian heritage from Eliza, her grandmother. She was taking part in the feasts she had heard about and she was seeing again the dances she remembered from her youth. Her parents had returned to Fairfax to live, which made the occasion even better.

That evening, at the Tallchief Theater in Fairfax, the chief of the Osage said solemnly, "Hereafter you, Maria Tallchief, will be known among the Osage as Princess Wa-Xthe-Thon-ba, Princess of Two Standards." It was the Osage way of saying that they knew she belonged to her mother's people as well as to them. Maria had tears in her eyes, for her mother had told her, "It was your grandmother who chose that name for you."

No ovation from an audience in New York or abroad had ever made Maria happier. She smiled to herself to think that now she really was the Indian princess the publicity department had tried to make her years ago! The evening was climaxed when the governor of Oklahoma made her a colonel on his staff and a commodore of the navy—which Oklahoma does not have!

That night Maria had a hard time getting to sleep. She had come home in more ways than one.

13. "The Closest to Perfection"

Maria was now every inch the dancer; she forced her spirit to rise above whatever might trouble her in her personal life. This effort made her a stronger and finer woman—and a still finer dancer. She had left her youth, her dependence on her parents and teachers. She had experienced love and unhappiness, and it all showed in her dancing.

Balanchine was aware of this and he knew the time was ripe for her to play a new role. "You will be the Sugar Plum Fairy," he said, "in *The Nutcracker*."

Maria loved the role. She felt it so strongly that she was the essence of the part—light and gay, seeming to float in air. The Balanchine version of the famous ballet, to the music of Tchaikovsky, has delighted children and grown-ups every year at Christmas since its first production in 1954.

With this role, considered the most difficult of all, a "new" Tallchief emerged. Walter Terry, the eminent dance critic, said that her artistry was enamel, not lacquer; diamond, not glass. Balanchine had created a masterpiece, but even he had always said that a true dancer is born, not made.

After *The Nutcracker*, Tallchief got a leave of absence to go with Ballet Russe on a tour of the United States. Audiences everywhere were afire to see Maria Tallchief, who was not only a great dancer, but also a great beauty. Her high cheekbones and brunette coloring, her mobile mouth and expressive eyes made her a striking person onstage and off. So great was her appeal that she was paid the highest salary—two thousand dollars a week—that any ballerina had ever been paid.

The tour was a series of triumphs. Ballet Russe

presented many of the numbers they had done countless times before, but with Tallchief's exquisite portrayals they became new and vivid. She was the fiery gypsy, the dreamy dryad in *Les Sylphides*, the love-sick Queen Zobeide in *Schéhérazade*. As Zobeide she stunned audiences with the passion and catlike grace of her interpretation, and left them moved to tears when she committed suicide. She was actress-dancer now, able to transmit all emotions to her audience and to combine these emotions with her flawless art.

Crisscrossing the country, she played in 103 cities, large and small. Critics and audiences alike acknowledged that she was the equal of the Russian Ulanova, the French Chauviré, the English Fonteyn. And she was American! When she played in Baltimore, motorcycle policemen had to clear a way for her to get to the station. She took uncounted curtain calls, her picture was everywhere, she was overwhelmed with flowers.

People all over the world clamored to see her—to know what this American Indian dancer could do, to compare her with their own ballerinas. And

Prima ballerina Maria Tallchief dancing the role of the Sugar Plum Fairy was especially appealing to children who flocked to holiday performances of *The Nutcracker* by the New York City Ballet.

everywhere she was acclaimed—in Europe, in Latin America, in Canada, in the Near East, in the Far East. Life became a constant round of performances, packing and unpacking suitcases, interviews, photographs, and admirers coming backstage to her dressing room.

It was an exciting, but a tiring, life. She was tempted to give it up, for she had fallen in love with a man who was very much in love with her. He was Henry D. Paschen, Jr., a Chicago businessman. For the first time, Maria knew that she was understood both as a woman and as a dancer. He would have liked her not to dance so much, but he believed that she must do what she needed to do. And Maria still needed to dance.

She married Mr. Paschen in 1956 and the next year appeared in a summer dance festival at the Ted Shawn Theatre in the Berkshires. The other featured dancer was Tom Two Arrows, an Iroquois. He danced the dances of his people, and Maria, the half-Indian, appeared in pink tutu and slippers in two numbers with André Eglevsky.

In 1958 Eglevsky left the New York City Ballet.

Balanchine had left, too—his wife, Tanaquil LeClercq, had been stricken with polio and he wished to be with her. There was a new director, new ballets, a new way of doing things that neither Tallchief nor Eglevsky enjoyed. So he decided to join the Long Island Academy of Dance, and Maria went home to Chicago to give birth to a baby daughter. Elise Maria was born in January 1959, a beautiful and delightful baby who became her mother's joy. Just the same, Maria was still obligated to her ballet company so, as soon as it was possible, she returned.

But now who would her partner be? Who could possibly equal Eglevsky? Fortune smiled on the company and on Maria, for Erik Bruhn, a Danish dancer, had been engaged. He had the build of an athlete and was blond and blue-eyed—a Viking of a man. Together, by the perfection of their dancing and the contrast in their appearance, they were unequaled. Everywhere they went they were acclaimed. After a short time, however, both resigned to join the American Ballet Theatre, touring in Europe and Russia.

Again it was a succession of triumphs. Maria was dancing more and more dramatic roles, proving not only her quality as a superb dancer but as an actress of depth and emotion. When they returned to New York in the spring of 1961, ballet lovers heard that she was to appear in *Miss Julie*, a ballet by Cullberg based on a play by Strindberg. There was a rush to buy tickets. What would she do with such a role? Miss Julie was a young woman of good family who falls in love with her butler; she is so bewitched by the affair that, little by little, she degrades herself until she commits suicide.

On opening night, with Bruhn playing the part of the butler, the dance lovers had their answer. Maria was haughty, impassioned, despairing— stunning in her vitality and range of feeling. Walter Terry summed it up in his review. "What can one say when faced with the closest to perfection that dancing mortals can achieve?"

Success and approval and the rewards of years of hard work were sweet to Maria Tallchief. She had had everything now—the honors, the flowers, the money, the admiration, and the praise. It was time to bask in the love of her husband and to enjoy her child, an adorable blonde sprite.

So in 1966 she decided to play that other great role which would demand all of her talent and her devotion ... that of wife and mother.

She has never regretted it. Her sister lives in New York and Paris and occasionally dances with various groups. Marjorie's sons have grown into tall, handsome young men.

Elise Maria studies ballet, "but is not much interested in it," her mother says. "She *is* interested in the piano and is very talented, an exceptionally good student. I would love for her to sing, but feel that she will veer toward a more academic career. She's an extremely sensitive, happy individual and her father and I hope that she will continue in the same path."

What lies ahead? Only time will tell. But Maria Tallchief has the double satisfaction of looking back on her own achievement as America's prima ballerina, and looking ahead to her gifted child's future.

Glossary

adagio: in an easy, graceful manner

ballerina: leading female dancer in a ballet company

ballet: a dance having graceful, expressive movements which often tell a story. It is performed onstage by a group of dancers.

ballet master: the person responsible for instruction and discipline in the ballet company. He rehearses and assigns parts to the dancers and also conducts classes for them.

barre: a horizontal bar used by dancers as support as they exercise. It is attached securely to the wall about three-and-a-half feet from the floor.

choreographer: a person who creates a dance

classic ballet: definite steps and movements that can be varied to provide the basic material from which all new ballets are made.

concerto: a piece of music that is written with three contrasting movements for a symphony orchestra and one or more soloists.

corps de ballet: dancers in large groups; the chorus

double pirouette: two complete turns of the body made on one foot

en pointe: toe dancing

fouetté: a whipping motion of the free leg propelling the dancer around on the supporting leg

impresario: one who manages or sponsors a ballet

maître: instructor, teacher

pas de deux: a dance for two people

pirouette: a complete turn of the body on one foot

premier danseur: leading male ballet dancer

prima ballerina: This title is awarded to one or more of a company's best soloist ballerinas, who, after years of hard work, have mastered ballet technique.

repertoire: a list of ballets, dramas, or operas that a company or individual has rehearsed and is ready to perform

tutu: a short ballet skirt revealing the entire leg

Index

144

Adèle deLeeuw says, "Children's stories are a natural occupation for me." When Adèle and her sister, Cateau, were small girls, they entertained each other telling stories. Storytelling became a career when the deLeeuws put their talents to work in the Plainfield, New Jersey public library. Their storyhours were so popular that Miss deLeeuw converted from storytelling to storywriting. Her published books now number 57 and have been translated into ten foreign languages and transcribed into Braille.

Her poems have been set to music, sung on the radio, made into records, and her stories have appeared in more than a hundred' magazines.